LOOKING AT COUNTRIES

Looking at
FRANCE

Jillian Powell

GARETH**STEVENS**
GS
PUBLISHING
A Member of the WRC Media Family of Companies

Please visit our web site at: www.garethstevens.com
For a free color catalog describing Gareth Stevens Publishing's list
of high-quality books and multimedia programs, call 1-800-542-2595 (USA)
or 1-800-387-3178 (Canada). Gareth Stevens Publishing's fax: (414) 332-3567.

Library of Congress Cataloging-in-Publication Data

Powell, Jillian.
　　Looking at France / Jillian Powell.
　　　　p. cm. — (Looking at countries)
　　Includes index.
　　ISBN-13: 978-0-8368-7668-0 (lib. bdg.)
　　ISBN-13: 978-0-8368-7675-8 (softcover)
　　1. France—Juvenile literature. I. Title.
　DC17.P78　2007
　944—dc22　　　　　　　2006034874

This North American edition first published in 2007 by
Gareth Stevens Publishing
A Member of the WRC Media Family of Companies
330 West Olive Street, Suite 100
Milwaukee, Wisconsin 53212 USA

This U.S. edition copyright © 2007 by Gareth Stevens, Inc.
Original edition copyright © 2006 by Franklin Watts.
First published in Great Britain in 2006 by Franklin Watts,
338 Euston Road, London NW1 3BH, United Kingdom.

Series editor: Sarah Peutrill
Art director: Jonathan Hair
Design: Rita Storey

Gareth Stevens editor: Dorothy L. Gibbs
Gareth Stevens art direction: Tammy West
Gareth Stevens graphic designer: Charlie Dahl

Photo credits: (t=top, b=bottom, l=left, r=right, c=center)
CORBIS: cover. Eric Brading/Alamy: 13. Dex Images/Corbis: 23. Bernd Ducke/Superbild/A1 Pix: 26c.
Owen Franken/Corbis: 12, 17. Gunter Gräfenhain/Superbild/A1 Pix: 8. Shaun Greenfield Photography/Photographers Direct: 11.
HAGA/Superbild/A1 Pix: 27. Chris Hellier/Corbis: 19. John Heseltine/Corbis: 21b. Roger G. Howard/Photographers Direct: 16.
Incolor/Superbild/A1 Pix: 7t. Buddy Mays/Photographers Direct: 20. Frederic Pitchal/Sygma/Corbis: 22. E. Poupinet/
Superbild/A1 Pix: 1,14. Roy Rainford/Robert Harding: 6, 7b. Walter Rawlings/Robert Harding: 21t. Sayama/Superbild/
A1 Pix: 9. Peter Scholey/Robert Harding: 4. Alex Segre/Photographers Direct: 25t. Sygma/Corbis: 26br. Guy Thouvenin/
Robert Harding: 18. Horacio Villalobos/Corbis: 10. Visa Image/Robert Harding: 25b. Tim de Waele/Corbis: 24.
Adam Woolfitt/Corbis: 15.

Every effort has been made to trace the copyright holders for the photos used in this book. The publisher apologizes,
in advance, for any unintentional omissions and would be pleased to insert the appropriate acknowledgements in any
subsequent edition of this publication.

Printed in Canada

1 2 3 4 5 6 7 8 9 10 10 09 08 07 06

Contents

Words that appear in the glossary are printed in **boldface** type the first time they occur in the text.

Where is France?

France is the largest country in western Europe. It is so large that it not only has two long coasts but also borders eight other European countries.

Paris is the capital city of France. It is a very old city on the Seine River, with many famous landmarks, including the Eiffel Tower and Notre Dame cathedral.

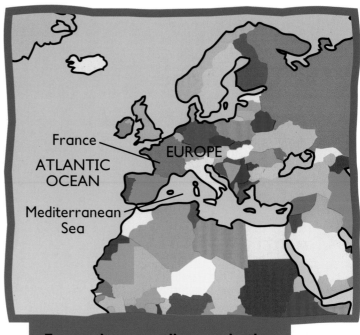

France
ATLANTIC
OCEAN
EUROPE
Mediterranean
Sea

France has coastlines on both sides of the country.

Notre Dame cathedral is on an island in the Seine River.

France does not share a land border with Great Britain, but the two countries are joined by an underwater tunnel that crosses the English Channel.

GREAT BRITAIN

BELGIUM

GERMANY

ENGLISH CHANNEL

•Le Touquet

LUXEMBOURG

Calvados   NORMANDY

PARIS ■   Seine River

BRITTANY

Le Mans •

FRANCE

BURGUNDY

• Dijon

SWITZERLAND

ATLANTIC OCEAN

Lyon

Chamonix

Alps   **ITALY**

• Rocamadour

Rhône River

PROVENCE

•Toulouse

• Arles

MONACO

Cannes

Pyrenees Mountains

FRENCH RIVIERA

SPAIN

ANDORRA

This map shows all the places that are mentioned in this book.

The Landscape

France has many different landscapes. It has gentle hills, flat plains, and lowland river valleys, as well as high mountain ranges, such as the Pyrenees and the Alps. In the south, the Mediterranean coastline has **salt flats** and **wetlands**, as well as sandy beaches.

The hill town of Rocamadour is built on the face of a rock cliff that rises high above a **gorge**.

Poplar trees line roads and rivers running through the rich farmland of northwestern France.

Many tourists visit France each year. Some come to see the countryside. Others enjoy the beautiful beaches on the south and west coasts.

The sunny coast in southern France is known as the French Riviera.

Did you know?

More than one-fourth of France is covered with forests.

Weather and Seasons

Most of France has cool winters and warm, sunny summers. The coldest winters are in the mountains, where heavy snow falls. The high mountains of the Alps shelter areas to the south from cold north winds, which keeps the French Riviera warm and sunny most of the year.

Winter snow makes the town of Chamonix, near Mont Blanc, a popular place for winter sports such as skiing and snowboarding.

Lavender grows well in the hot, sunny weather of Provence.

Along the Mediterranean coast, summers are usually hot and dry. Summer **droughts** often lead to forest fires. Rain falls mainly in the spring and autumn. Sometimes, a cold wind called the **mistral** blows over southern France, especially down the Rhône valley.

Did you know?

The mistral can blow so hard that it sometimes damages fields of crops.

French People

The people of France are a mix of different **cultures**. They come from Portugal, Russia, the Middle East, Asia, and North Africa.

France also has people of many different religions. Most are Roman Catholics, but there are some Muslims and small groups of Protestants and Jews, too.

This French woman is lighting prayer candles in a Roman Catholic church.

Popular regional foods are sold at farmers' markets throughout France.

Each region of France has its own traditional foods and **folk costumes**. The French language is spoken everywhere, but the people of some regions also speak local languages. Basque and Catalan are local languages in parts of France that are near the border of Spain. Breton is a local language in Brittany.

Did you know?

The French language is spoken in twenty-one other countries of the world.

School and Family

Children in France start school when they are six years old and continue going to school until they are sixteen to eighteen years old. The school day starts at 8:30 a.m. and ends at 5:30 p.m. Some schools have Wednesday afternoons free so children can take part in sports activities or youth clubs.

In most French schools, students do not wear special clothing or uniforms.

French families enjoy spending time together and often invite relatives to join them for birthday parties and other special family celebrations.

French schools give their students a two-hour lunch break. Some children eat lunch at school. Others go home to eat lunch with their families, then return to finish the school day.

Home and family life are important in France. The French government helps families to make sure they have good housing and that children receive good care. The government also tries to make sure that parents have time to spend with their children, both at home and in the schools.

Country Life

Only about one-fourth of the people in France live in countryside villages or small market towns. As more people have moved to the cities to find work, many country and farm houses have become second homes or vacation homes for city people or tourists. Many of these houses are hundreds of years old.

Grapes have been grown in France for more than one thousand years. The Burgundy region in east-central France has many vineyards.

The Calvados area in the northern region of Normandy has many old, country-style houses.

Many French market towns are built around a main square, usually with a church, a town hall, and some small shops on the square. Most of these towns also have an outdoor market at least once a week.

City Life

Most people in France live in large towns or big cities. Paris is the biggest city. It is also the country's capital city, which means that it is the center of French government. Like most big cities, Paris has fashionable shops, cafés, and restaurants, as well as large office buildings, factories, art galleries, and museums.

Motorbikes are a popular means of transportation in French cities.

Paris has an underground train system, called the "metro" (short for *Metropolitain*), that makes getting around the city very easy.

Paris is a center of the fashion industry. Cannes, a city on the Mediterranean coast, is famous for the international film festival held there each year. Other large cities in France are important for their local industries, such as clothmaking in Lyon or aircraft **manufacturing** in Toulouse.

Did you know?

In central Paris, every building is only about 1,500 feet (450 meters) from a metro station.

French Houses

Many French people live in blocks of apartment buildings in the **suburbs** of cities and travel into the cities to work. Some of the apartment buildings in France are newly built, modern **high-rises**. Others are more than one hundred years old.

Did you know?

The most magnificent houses in France are the *châteaux*, or castles. Many of them were built in the 1500s.

The balconies of these high-rise apartments in Le Touquet have a view of the English Channel.

Some of the houses in Arles, in the region of Provence, were built in Roman or medieval times.

Older houses in French towns and villages are usually built of stone and have clay-tile roofs and shutters at the windows. Many of these houses have three or more stories, and some are built in **terraces**.

19

French Food

People in France shop for food at supermarkets each week, but they also like to buy fresh foods from street markets and small stores such as cheese shops and bakeries.

Some people in France visit markets daily to buy bread and other fresh foods.

Many French restaurants and cafés have tables outdoors for customers who enjoy eating in the open air.

France is world-famous for its foods and cooking. Many regions of France are known for particular foods and dishes, such as mustard from Dijon, snails from Burgundy, fish soups and stews from Provence, and **crepes** from Brittany.

The northern region of Normandy is famous for dishes using local foods such as apples and cream.

At Work

Throughout France, people work in banks, shops, offices, and schools. Some people work in factories, making cars, perfumes, wines, or cheeses that are sold worldwide. The main industries in France include machinery, aircraft and other transportation equipment, **textiles**, and **electronics**.

Cars made in France are sold all over the world.

Many tourists come to France for its fine foods and elegant restaurants.

In Paris and other historic cities and towns, and at coastal **resorts**, large numbers of tourists create lots of jobs in hotels, restaurants, and shops. Tourist attractions, such as art galleries and museums, also provide jobs.

Did you know?

More than sixty million tourists visit France each year.

23

Having Fun

Popular sports in France include soccer, tennis, auto races, and cycling. Each year, France hosts international events such as the French Open tennis tournament, the Grand Prix auto race at Le Mans, and the *Tour de France* bicycle race.

Cyclists come to France from all over the world to compete in the famous *Le Tour de France* bicycle race.

Boules, which is a kind of outdoor bowling, is a popular game in towns and villages all over France.

French people also enjoy movies, plays, and art shows.

France has holidays and festivals all through the year. People often wear folk costumes for these events and celebrate with singing, dancing, and feasting.

Did you know?

France has more than four hundred festivals. Some celebrate foods, such as sausages, snails, or frogs' legs.

This woman is dressed in a Breton folk costume for a religious festival in Brittany.

France: The Facts

- Almost sixty-one million people live in France. More than two million of them live in Paris.

- France is a **republic**. The president is the **head of state**, and the prime minister leads the government.

- The island of Corsica, off the western coast of Italy, and some overseas territories, such as the Caribbean islands of Guadaloupe and Martinique, are also part of France.

- France is a member of the European Union.

The French flag is sometimes called the "tricolor," or three-color, because it has three equal bands of color — red, white, and blue.

France uses the European currency euros and cents. This coin shows the back of the one-cent French euro.

The Eiffel Tower in Paris is lit up with fireworks to celebrate July 14, 1790, the day that France became a republic.

Did you know?

The name *France* comes from the Franks, the people who lived there after the end of the Roman Empire.

Glossary

crepes – paper-thin pancakes

cultures – specific groups or nations of people that share the same basic backgrounds and beliefs within each group

droughts – long periods of time without rain that are harmful to plants and animals in the area

electronics – equipment and parts of equipment that are made using electron or computer technology

folk costumes – special kinds of clothing that are passed down through generations in a particular country

gorge – a deep, narrow canyon or passage with steep sides

head of state – the main representative of a country

high-rises – very tall buildings with elevators

manufacturing – making something in a factory

medieval times – the Middle Ages, between about the fifth and fifteenth centuries

mistral – a strong, cold wind that blows down from the Alps across southern France

republic – a kind of government in which decisions are made by the people of the country and their representatives

resorts – places, usually close to bodies of water, that have food, lodging, and entertainment for vacationing visitors

Roman – from the culture of ancient Rome

salt flats – flat, salt-crusted areas of land left behind when bodies of saltwater dry up

suburbs – areas outside of large cities, made up mostly of homes where people live, instead of places where people work

terraces – steplike levels or layers

textiles – threads, yarns, and woven cloths, or fabrics

vineyards – places where grapevines are planted

wetlands – low, marshy or swampy areas of land

Find Out More

France Homework Links (for Children)
www.woodlands-junior.kent.sch.uk/homework/france.html

Fun French
www.primaryfrench.co.uk

Time for Kids: France
www.timeforkids.com/TFK/hh/goplaces/main/
    0,20344,491045,00.html

Welcome to France
www.info-france-usa.org/kids/

Publisher's note to educators and parents: Our editors have carefully reviewed these Web sites to ensure that they are suitable for children. Many Web sites change frequently, however, and we cannot guarantee that a site's future contents will continue to meet our high standards of quality and educational value. Be advised that children should be closely supervised whenever they access the Internet.

My Map of France

Photocopy or trace the map on page 31. Then write in the names of the countries, bodies of water, regions, cities, and land areas and mountains listed below. (Look at the map on page 5 if you need help.)

After you have written in the names of all the places, find some crayons and color the map!

Countries
France
Great Britain
Italy
Spain

Bodies of Water
Atlantic Ocean
English Channel
Mediterranean Sea
Rhône River
Seine River

Regions
Brittany
Burgundy
Normandy
Provence

Cities
Arles
Cannes
Chamonix
Dijon
Le Mans
Le Touquet
Lyon
Paris
Rocamadour
Toulouse

Land Areas and Mountains
Alps
French Riviera
Mont Blanc
Pyrenees Mountains

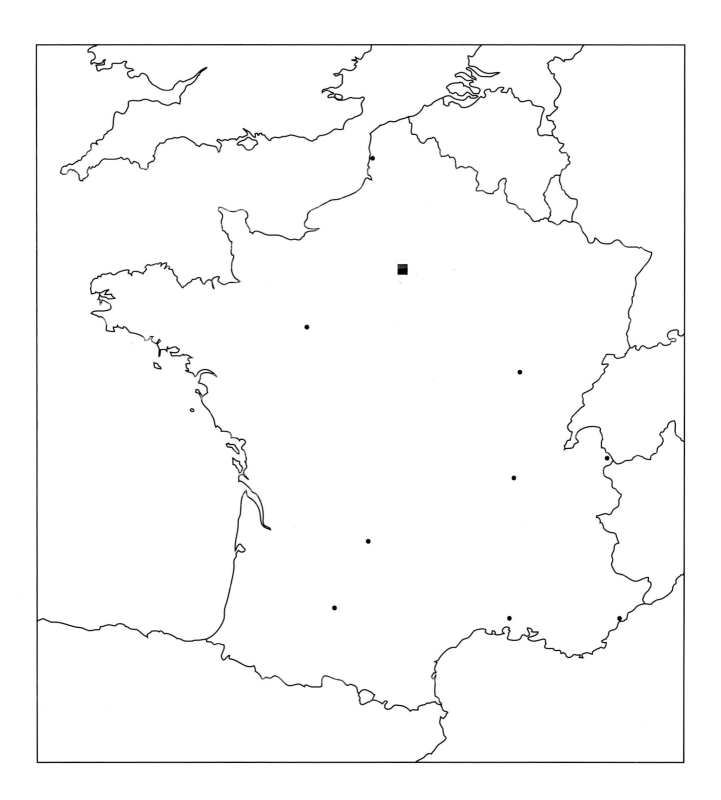

Index